MEGATECH

Cloning

Frontiers of genetic engineering

David Jefferis

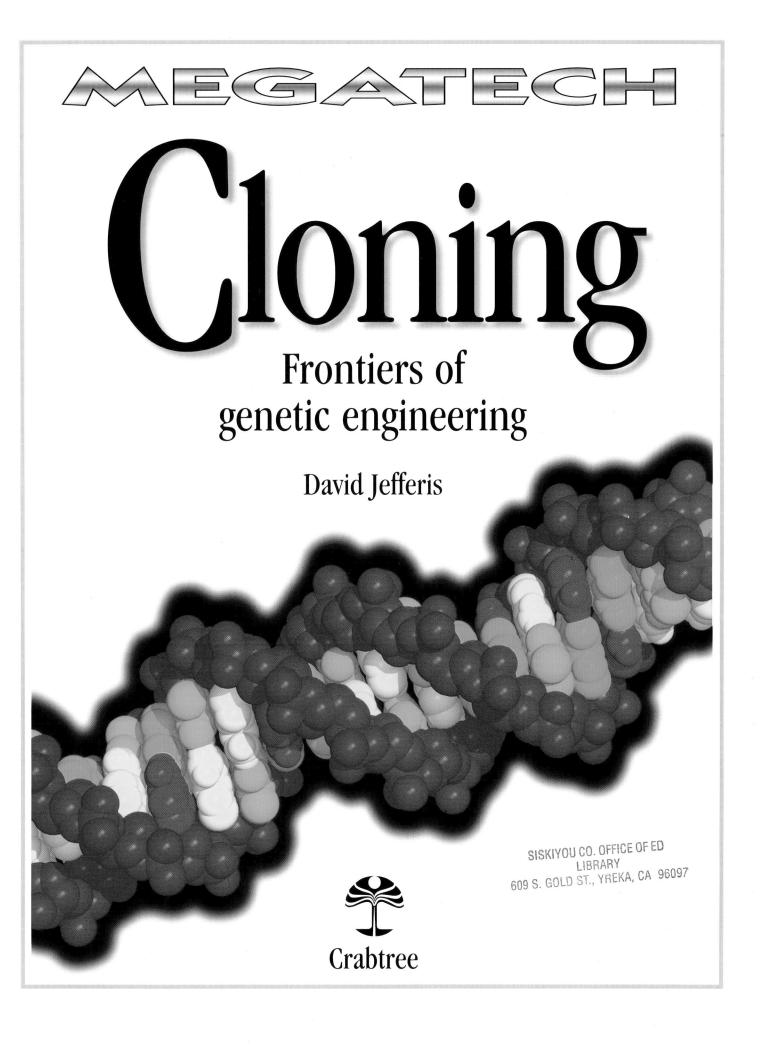

Crabtree

Introduction

Cloning is the creation of a living thing that is identical to, or a 'clone,' of a single parent. Some simple plants and animals reproduce this way. Human clones happen in nature as identical twins. Today, scientists are beginning to make clones to order. Cloning is an area of science called genetic engineering.

Developments in cloning research make newspaper headlines almost every day. The purpose of the research is to change all sorts of living things ('organisms') to provide people with better health, drugs, and food.

The success of genetic engineering, and cloning in particular, reveals a future for humanity which is full of promise, yet which has some frightening prospects, too. Read about both sides of the question in these pages.

MEGATECH

Crabtree Publishing Company
PMB 16A   612 Welland Ave
350 Fifth Ave   St. Catharines, ON
Ste. 3308   Canada L2M 5V6
New York
NY 10118

234567 Printed in Belgium 76543210

Edited by
Norman Barrett
Coordinating editor
Ellen Rodger
Consulting Editor
Virgina Mainprize

Technical consultant
Gerard Cheshire BSc
Picture research by
David Pratt

Created and produced by
Alpha Communications in association
with Firecrest Books Ltd.

©1999 Alpha Communications and
©1999 Firecrest Books Ltd.

Cataloging-in-Publication Data
Jefferis, David.
    Cloning: frontiers of genetic
engineering / David Jefferis; technical
consultant, Gerard Cheshire.
        p. cm. -- (Megatech)
    Includes index.

    Summary: Discusses the science of
genetics, the first successful cloning of
a mammal, its implications and its
ethical aspects.

ISBN 0-7787-0058-5 (paper). --
ISBN 0-7787-0048-8(rlb)
    1. Cloning--Juvenile literature. 2.
Genetic engineering--Juvenile
literature. 3. Medical genetics--Juvenile
literature.
[1. Cloning. 2. Genetic engineering.] I.
Title. II. Series.
QH442.2.J44 1999
571.8'918--dc21 LC 98-48513
CIP AC

Pictures on these pages,
clockwise from far left:
1 Possible human
clones.
2 Genetically modified
tomato plants.
3 Genetic researcher
checks on cloned bacteria.
4 Dolly the cloned sheep.
5 Genes of a fruit fly.
6 DNA profiling.

Previous page shows:
Computer image of DNA.

Color separation by
Job Color, Italy
Printed in Belgium by
Casterman Printers

Contents

Genes and clones

Cloning is one aspect of genetic engineering, the rapidly growing area of scientific research that tries to change and control the design of living things.

To understand cloning, you need to know about the smallest parts of living things. In every one of the billions of tiny cells that make up the body, there are groups of chemicals called 'genes.' Each gene is a set of instructions that controls how a protein is made. There are thousands of different proteins. They carry out the work of the body, from breaking down food for energy, to helping brain cells communicate with each other.

Genetic engineering can remove some gene instructions from one cell and place them in another. A plant may be given genes to resist disease carried by insects. An animal may have genes added to help it stay healthy.

▲ *The hydra is a small animal that lives in ponds. A baby hydra grows on the side of its parent. Soon it breaks away to live by itself. The two hydras have exactly the same genes, so they are clones.*

A clone is a living thing that has exactly the same genes as its parent. In sexual reproduction, genes from both male and female parents are mixed to create children that have genes from both their father and mother. A clone has the genes of only one parent, so it is identical to the parent. Many plants, and some very simple animals, reproduce by cloning. However, genetic engineering has now made it possible to clone more complex animals, such as frogs, sheep, and cows.

▲ *Genes are in the dark stripes of these hugely enlarged curly objects called 'chromosomes.' These are chromosomes of a housefly.*

▼ *To grow a new banana tree, a farmer simply cuts off a new shoot and plants it. The new banana has identical genes to its parent plant, so it is a clone.*

▶ *Many plants reproduce in two ways. Strawberries have flowers, which make seeds for sexual reproduction. Strawberry plants may also send out 'runners,' which form new plants by themselves.*

▶ Researchers in Scotland created a cloned sheep in 1996. The animal, named Dolly, was a big step for genetic engineering. It was the first clone of such a complex animal. Read the story of Dolly on page 14.

It took researchers nearly 300 tries before they succeeded with Dolly

The secrets of genes, and how to control them, were once a complete mystery. The invention of the microscope in 1608, helped scientists find out what living things are made of, and how they work.

Mice were cloned in 1998 by researchers based in Hawaii

◀ The sea anemone normally lays eggs, but can also reproduce by cloning. An adult anemone splits in two, and the two halves slowly move away from each other. When they have grown to full size again, they split once more. In this way an entire colony may be formed, every anemone a clone of the original animal.

Are there drawbacks to cloning?

Reproduction without mixing genes has one big problem. Because all cloned living things are the same as their parent, they share the same strengths and weaknesses. If disease strikes and one clone is infected, they all could be infected.

With sexual reproduction, the variety of genes in any group of plants or animals usually means that some will escape the disease.

Life changes

▲ *Charles Darwin's ship set off in December 1831 on a long mission to map the coast of South America. Collecting plant and animal specimens was an important part of the exploration.*

The science of genetic engineering has its roots in the experience of farmers who have been breeding animals for thousands of years.

Genetic engineering is a new science, yet it is not so different from the breeding done by farmers for thousands of years. Even though no one knew why a particular cow gave very creamy milk, farmers discovered that breeding from the best milkers gradually improved a herd.

▲ *Charles Darwin (1809-82) was one of the pioneers of evolution theory. His grandfather, Erasmus, had earlier suggested that living things adapted to changes in their environment.*

◄ *Farm and domestic animals have long been bred to suit human needs.*

Other animals – horses, pigs, sheep, dogs, and many others – have also been improved by selective breeding. Farmers know that by planting seeds from their best plants, they can have tasty fruit or bumper crops.

It was not until the first fossil-hunters found remains of long-extinct creatures such as dinosaurs that the idea of living things changing naturally over time began to be accepted.

Charles Darwin was one of a group of scientists and others who found that living things could change over time, without the assistance of humans. During a five-year voyage (1831-36) as ship's naturalist on the HMS Beagle, Darwin visited the Galapagos Islands in the Pacific Ocean, 600 miles (965 km) from South America.

Darwin found fossil remains of extinct animals and collected plants and animals that no one had ever seen before. Among these were 'Darwin's finches,' thirteen different types of the same bird. Each type lived on its own island and had a different shape and size of beak.

▲ *An early edition of Charles Darwin's famous book 'On the Origin of Species.'*

◀ The Galapagos Islands have many unique and interesting creatures, including these giant iguanas.

▼ The finch below uses a twig to dig out insects from holes in a tree branch. No wonder Darwin found finches so fascinating!

Darwin had an idea, or theory, to explain why the birds were different. He thought that one type, or species, of finch had once flown from mainland South America to the islands. Isolated on the separate islands, their descendants gradually changed, or evolved, to suit conditions on each particular island. Some birds developed sharp beaks for opening seeds, others acquired larger beaks for eating insects.

For many years, Darwin developed his ideas on how this process of change might work. Finally, in 1859, he published his results in a book called On the Origin of Species. It showed that life on Earth seems to have evolved from earlier forms.

What is natural selection?

Darwin's theory was that conditions in the wild 'selected' creatures that could survive best.

Plants or animals best suited to their environment had the best chance of survival.

If the environment changed, only plants and animals that could cope would survive. Darwin thought that at one time all the finches on the Galapgos Islands were the same type. Over thousands of years, the birds on different islands slowly changed, or evolved, depending on the conditions on each island.

Darwin concluded that eventually such gradual changes could lead to entirely new species.

Genetic dawn

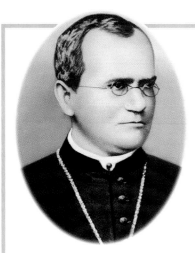

▲ *Gregor Mendel's work laid the foundations of genetics despite his research being ignored for many years. He gave up his experiments in 1868, when he became abbot of the monastery.*

The man who set the scene for genetics was an Austrian monk called Gregor Mendel. He bred plants for many years in a monastery garden, where he studied them carefully.

Gregor Mendel was born in 1822, at Heinzendorf in Austrian Silesia (now in the Czech Republic). When he was 25, he became a priest at Brunn monastery and went off to Vienna University to train as a teacher. He returned to the monastery, and in 1856, he started an eight-year series of breeding experiments with plants. His aim was to see how different features were passed from parent plants to their offspring.

Mendel used pea plants for various experiments

Mendel decided to study plant characteristics, such as tallness and shortness, color of seeds, and smooth or wrinkled seeds. He fertilized plants by taking pollen from flower to flower, just as insects do in the wild. He found definite patterns in the young plants that grew from these seeds and decided that plants must have what he called 'particles of inheritance.'

Soon, Mendel could predict how many plants would be tall, how many short, and so on.

▲ *Creating splendid new or mixed (hybrid) varieties has been the aim of keen gardeners for centuries. Today's commercial flower growers tempt buyers with large, brightly colored blooms that last a long time.*

◄ *Bonsai, the art of miniature trees, started in Japan centuries ago. Tiny trees result from the careful pruning of roots. Even so, their seeds do not change. If you plant a bonsai's seed in open ground, in a few years you should have a full-size tree.*

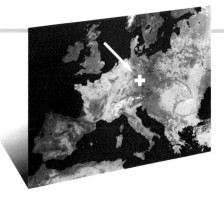

◄ *Gregor Mendel's monastery was built in eastern Europe, in what is now the Czech Republic. Mendel was a monk of the Augustinian order. Brunn (white cross on this map) has since been renamed and is now called Brno.*

▲ *For his experiments, Mendel pollinated test plants by hand. In the wild, bright colors and scent attract insects, which take pollen to other plants. This method mixes genes between plants at random and is good for keeping a species strong and healthy. It is not so good if a grower wishes to develop precise color or other characteristics.*

Mendel was correct with his theory of 'particles,' which today are known as genes. He thought that each plant had a pair of particles for each characteristic, one from each parent. Mendel suggested that some characteristics, such as tallness, were more powerful, or 'dominant.' Others, such as shortness, were less powerful, or 'recessive.' Even so, the recessive genes did not disappear. They could come back in later generations of plants.

Mendel gave genetics a good start, but his work was overlooked at first. His work was published in the Brunn Natural Scientific Society's journal in 1865, but it was not until 1900, 16 years after his death, that Mendel's achievements were recognized.

What is a polygene?

Mendel had a fairly simple task in his experiments, because his work with plants involved just single genes.

A polygene is more complicated. It is a group of genes that works as a team and may control things such as the color of skin or body weight.

Single genes in a polygene can be studied, but, like the runners in a relay race, it is the result of the group's action that counts.

Exploring the cell

Like bricks that make up a wall, cells are the basic units of all living things, from tiny bacteria to giant oaks, from sea slugs to human beings.

▲ *Robert Hooke's studies covered a number of subjects, from fleas to leaves, but his microscopes did not give huge enlargements in comparison to today's powerful microscopes.*

Before Mendel's experiments, scientists, using microscopes, had explored the world of the very small. English physicist Robert Hooke was among the first to use the microscope for serious scientific work. The instrument had been invented by Zacharias Jansen, of Holland, in 1608, before Hooke was born in 1635.

Hooke published a book called Micrographia, which means 'small drawings.' In 1665, he showed that a thin slice of cork was made of "a great many little boxes." He called them cells, after the compartments of a bee honeycomb, which he thought looked similar.

Robert Hooke lived long before cameras were invented, so he made drawings of specimens, including this flea

▶ *Right, one of Hooke's carefully labeled drawings, a twig and leaf. Above, the type of closeup view his microscope showed of plant cells.*

Other scientists joined in to investigate the invisible world that the microscope revealed. In 1831, Robert Brown from Scotland discovered that plant cells have a small object inside. He called this center of the cell, the nucleus.

Soon, three German scientists added new findings to the study of cells. In 1838, Matthias Schlieden saw that other plants were also made of cells. A year later, Theodor Schwann put forward the 'cell theory.' Schwann thought that animals are also made of cells. He was convinced that each cell is a living thing, and that complex organisms such as humans are made of many cells, acting as a group. Scientist Carl von Siebold went back to basics. He saw that some of the tiniest organisms are made of just a single cell, which also has a nucleus.

▶ *Unlike those of animals, plant cells have an outer wall made of cellulose. The nucleus carries genes of what Mendel called "particles of inheritance."*

Cell wall

Nucleus

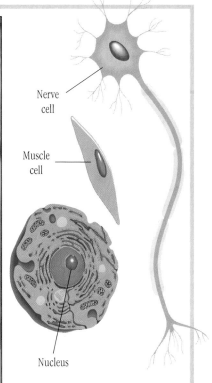

Nerve cell

Muscle cell

Nucleus

▲ *Cells come in all shapes and sizes. They carry out different jobs in the body. Complex plants are also made up of many different types of cells. They all have a nucleus containing genetic material.*

◄ *Electron microscopes can magnify more than a million times, They can produce images of a tiny universe invisible to the naked eye.*

W ith these discoveries, the secrets of the cell were being unlocked. Further research involved cell division, which is the process by which living things grow.

How do cells divide?

Cell division or 'mitosis,' is the way an organism grows. The nucleus splits in two, and two new 'daughter' cells result. Each cell is the same as its parent. As this process repeats, the organism gets bigger.

Male and female sex cells divide in a process called 'meiosis.' When male and female sex cells join together, genetic material from the nucleus of each is mixed. The result is an offspring with a mixture of each parent's characteristics.

◄ *A cell at the moment of division. The very bright colors shown here are not real. The cells are colored to show details in the picture.*

The plan of life

▲ *James Watson (left) and Francis Crick revealed the shape of the DNA molecule in 1953.*

Inside the nucleus, or core, of every cell are the things that control how living organisms work – chromosomes, DNA, and genes.

To the pioneer researchers in genetics, investigating the nucleus was like exploring a new world. Inside this world, they found tiny, thread-like chromosomes, which contain genes, or what Gregor Mendel called 'particles of inheritance.'

▼ *Computerized view of the spiral shape of DNA.*

Base pairs

A chromosome is made mostly of the molecule DNA, short for 'deoxyribonucleic acid.' DNA molecules are the message carriers for thousands upon thousands of chemical patterns, or sequences. These patterns are the genes, which together make up the plan of life.

DNA consists of two strands, which form a spiral called a 'double helix.' Like a ladder, the strands are joined by rungs, known as 'base pairs.' These base pairs, or genes, are the various code messages that define each living thing. Gene sequences provide the instructions for everything in nature, from the blue of a kingfisher's feathers to the length of an elephant's trunk.

▶ *Inside the nucleus of each cell are the genetic instructions that rule life. DNA in the chromosomes carries these instructions as patterns of gene sequences.*

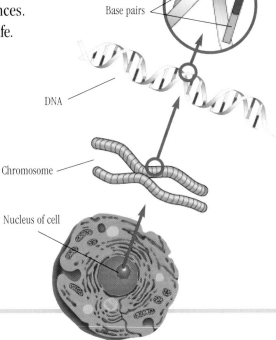

Base pairs

DNA

Chromosome

Nucleus of cell

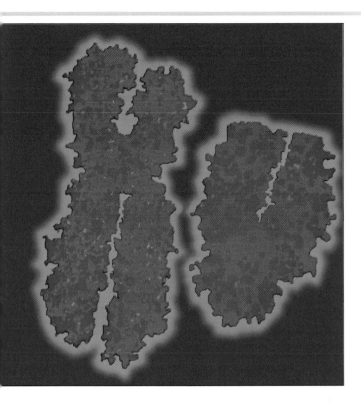

▶ *When cells divide, DNA strands are used as guides in creating new ones. The DNA unravels while new material forms a new strand, identical to the original.*

Base pairs

DNA unwinds

New DNA copy   New DNA copy

▲ *There are 46 chromosomes in each human cell. The 23rd pair, shown here, control whether you are a boy or a girl. Males have an 'X' and a 'Y' chromosome (above). Females have two 'X' chromosomes.*

D NA is a very effective message carrier. Just as the 26 letters of the alphabet can be arranged to make millions of different words, the genes in DNA can carry a large amount of information. In a human cell, each DNA molecule has about three billion base pairs, or genes, paving the way for countless genetic instruction groups.

If the DNA strands in just one human cell were stretched out in a line, they would measure about 36 inches long (91 cm). There are billions of cells in the human body!

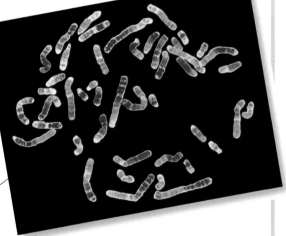

▼ *The color of eyes, blonde or brunette hair, fair or dark skin – these and all other characteristics are controlled by the genes. Originally, they come from the sex cells of parents. Each parent gives its child half of the genetic material that makes the child unique.*

Human chromosomes, shown enlarged about 2500 times

What is CGTA?

These are the initial letters of the four molecules that make up the base pairs strung between the curling double helix 'spines' of DNA.

Different groupings of these molecules – cytosine, guanine, thymine and adenine (CGTA) – control the chemical processes inside a cell.

Using this basically simple system, DNA is in charge of the elements of life itself.

Dolly the clone

T he year 1996 saw a scientific breakthrough that few people had expected so early. It was the cloning of a sheep, an animal much more complex than simple plants or bacteria.

▲ Lamb number 6LL3, named Dolly, made big news. Scientists dealt with 2000 telephone calls, nearly 100 reporters, 16 film crews and over 50 photographers.

To create the sheep, a team of scientists from Scotland, led by researcher Ian Wilmut, took a single cell from the udder of a female sheep. They joined this to an unfertilized egg cell from another sheep, having first removed all genetic material from the egg. The joined cells grew into an embryo, which was then put into the womb of a third sheep. From there on, pregnancy and birth were normal. When born, the lamb (named Dolly) was also perfectly normal, except that she had no father. She was exactly like the sheep from whose udder the cell had been taken.

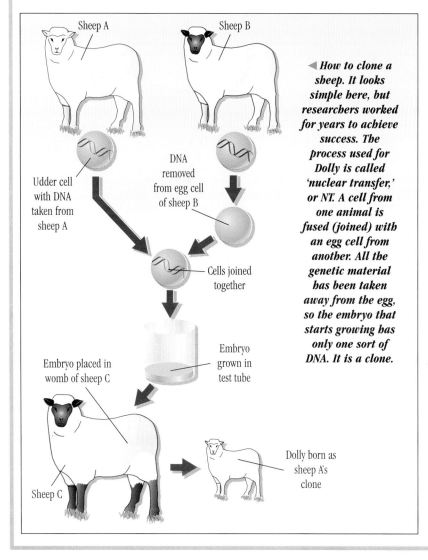

Sheep A

Sheep B

Udder cell with DNA taken from sheep A

DNA removed from egg cell of sheep B

Cells joined together

Embryo grown in test tube

Embryo placed in womb of sheep C

Sheep C

Dolly born as sheep A's clone

◀ How to clone a sheep. It looks simple here, but researchers worked for years to achieve success. The process used for Dolly is called 'nuclear transfer,' or NT. A cell from one animal is fused (joined) with an egg cell from another. All the genetic material has been taken away from the egg, so the embryo that starts growing has only one sort of DNA. It is a clone.

Embryo

Point of pin

▶ An early embryo is a tiny cluster of cells, small enough to fit on the point of a pin, as shown in this microscope picture. Cell division continues, and the embryo develops. A sheep embryo takes about 20 weeks from fertilization to birth, compared with nine months for a human.

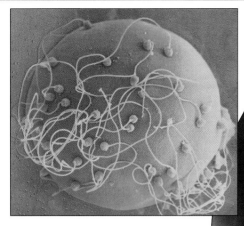

▲ *Fertilization the traditional way: here male sperm cells cluster round a female egg cell. Only one of the sperms will penetrate the egg for fertilization to take place.*

▶ *Genetic research is a 'clean-room' job. Sensitive lab equipment can be wrecked if contaminated by foreign particles.*

Other animals have also been cloned

The unusual thing about Dolly's cloning was that the udder cell was fully grown. Normally, adult cells are 'differentiated.' This means that, as an embryo develops, cells specialize, forming udder, nose, foot, or other body parts. For cloning to work, Ian Wilmut's research team had to make the cell 'young' again. Part of the procedure was to almost starve it. This process made the egg cell believe it was meeting a young cell, and so the growth process was begun. Why the near-starvation plan worked is not fully understood.

Clones of more animals have been made since Dolly, including mice and calves. Dolly gave birth to a lamb, Bonnie, in 1998. Bonnie seemed normal, which encouraged the research team to consider using their 'nuclear transfer' method in other ways. Future plans include modifying pigs' organs to use as 'spare parts' for humans who need new hearts, livers, or other organs.

What is fertilization?

This is the word for the meeting of male and female sex cells during reproduction.

In humans and other mammals, a male sperm joins with, or fertilizes, a female egg. This fertilization begins a new life.

Genetic material from the sperm and egg mix to create a new set of DNA instructions. The fertilized egg cell divides and grows, and soon an embryo (unborn infant) is growing in the female's womb.

Cracking the code

Discovering all the secrets of DNA is an international project, involving scientists across the world. Scientists are sharing the results of their research into the nature and make-up of chromosomes.

▲ Variations in DNA account for the differences between organisms.

The genome is the name for all the genes in any species, or type, of plant or animal. Finding out about human genes is the aim of HUGO, the Human Genome Organization. It is a worldwide project which links together more than 1000 scientists in 50 countries.

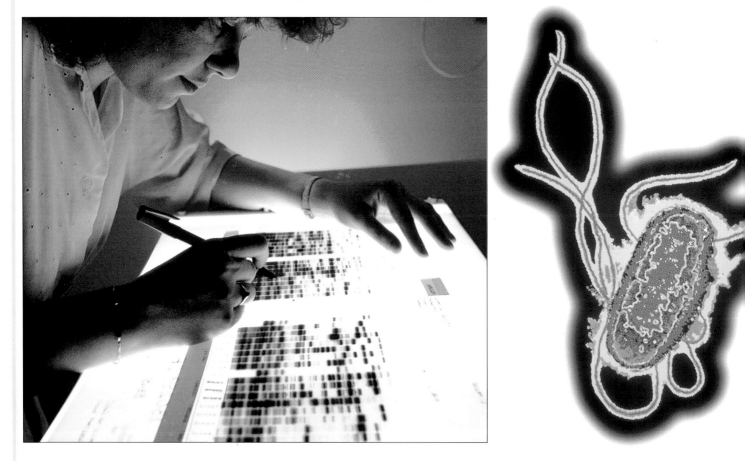

▲ DNA patterns vary between people, and a way of showing this is in DNA profiling. It is a useful technique in investigating crimes. By matching the DNA in the hair, blood, or skin cells, with those taken at crime scenes, scientists can tell if a suspect is guilty.

There are about three billion genes in human DNA, although only 50,000 to 100,000 seem to be actively involved in sending messages. No one yet knows what the rest are for. Progress on the genome project has been rapid, and by 1998, over 6000 genes had been identified.

These discoveries included genes that may cause epilepsy, drug addiction, and brain damage. Identifying a gene sequence is only the first part of the story and is probably the easy part. The difficult task that follows each discovery is to find out how the gene works in the body.

▲ E.coli, the food-poisoning organism, is enlarged in this image produced by an electron microscope.

What is a mutation?

Sometimes genetic instructions are damaged or are not copied perfectly from adult to offspring. Such a change in the genes is known as a mutation.

Most mutations are too small to be noticed. Others cause dramatic changes. This is how evolution can work in 'sudden jumps.' The 'sudden jump' idea was first suggested by Dutch botanist Hugo de Vries, back in the 1800s.

◄ *A two-headed turtle is not the sort of creature you meet every day, even on the Galapagos Islands. It is a mutant, with damaged genes.*

Mutants were a feature of 1950s science fiction stories. In the movie 'Them,' giant ants resulted from genetic changes caused by atomic bomb radiation

S cience teams have worked on the genomes of all sorts of living things, including human beings, worms, flies, apples, and barley. Bacteria are simple organisms, and by 1998 the genomes of more than 20 bacteria were known. They include one that your family doctor probably knows quite well – Escherichia coli. It is better known simply as E. coli, and some strains cause severe food poisoning. There have been many illnesses, and even deaths, caused by E. coli.

Discovering the genomes of different organisms has revealed that all living things use variations of DNA and has shown how closely linked the life forms are on our planet.

◄ *Giraffes, snakes, eagles, and other living things all have DNA coding to pass on their genes to offspring.*

Cloning people

Experimenting with human beings is the next step in cloning. Some genetic researchers have pointed out that there are many problems with cloning people.

▲ Cloning researchers point out that even perfect-looking 'natural' babies may have many genetic defects. These can result in illnesses that show up only later in life.

Cloning is not that unusual. Gardeners have been cloning plants for centuries, without knowing anything about the science involved. Genetic engineers have also been cloning living things for many years, but experiments have been mostly on simple organisms such as bacteria.

▶ The movie 'Gattaca' showed a future in which the natural-born hero fights to survive in a world filled with cloned humans and genetically perfect super beings. In a world such as this, normal humans could become slaves to these new bosses.

▼ Tiny samples of blood from a blood bank, or stray hairs with roots in a comb may provide enough cells to create a clone.

Dolly the sheep changed things because she was the first clone of such a complex creature. The experiments were mostly made for money-making purposes. If you have one valuable animal, perhaps a sheep with fine-quality wool, you can clone a flock of exactly the same sheep. Doing these experiments with humans raises many difficult questions.

Most experts think that this type of cloning technology is too dangerous for use with humans. However, it is only a matter of time before someone tries it out.

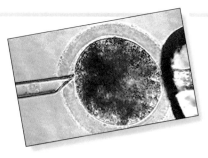

▲ *Cloning technology is a very delicate science. Special micro-size equipment has been developed to deal with tiny cells.*

▶ *Bacteria containing cloned DNA are inspected in a laboratory. Methods used to clone Dolly the sheep were used with other creatures, too. By 1998, researchers had succeeded in cloning other complex organisms, including mice and calves. Experts believe a human could be cloned soon.*

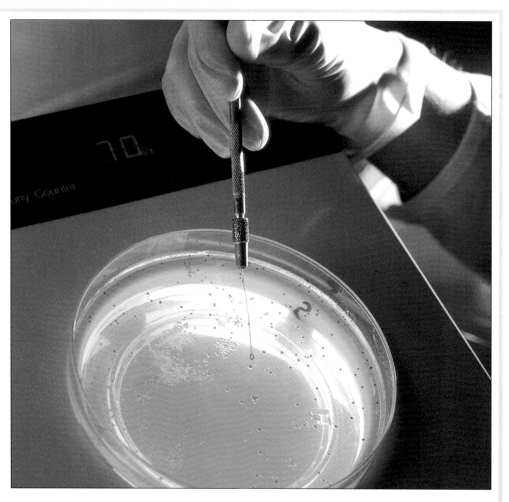

If you had a clone, would it be an identical twin? The answer is: yes and no. Like identical twins who are separated at birth, the clone might look and behave somewhat like you, but it would not be you. Like you, the clone would be an individual and would act as an individual, even if it was raised in a similar environment.

People outside the medical world are also interested in human cloning research. One group believes that humans were cloned by extraterrestrial visitors in prehistoric times. Other work includes the cloning of family pets. If your pet dies, you could pay to have it recreated as a clone. In 1998, a U.S. millionaire paid a research team $5 million to try to clone his dog!

◀ *Pet cloning is a possible for the future, but will a parrot clone talk as well as its parent?*

Danger – clones ahead?

Cloning is a new technology, and many people say it is best to take a breather before rushing ahead too fast, especially with humans.

Certainly, there are many things to find out. For example, no one knows exactly how the aging process works. If you were cloned at the age of 40, your clone might be born with 40 years of genetic damage, or have a lifespan cut short by that amount.

There are still many questions to answer, so further research and experiments with human cloning are best carried out with great care.

Organ transplants

▲ *Dr. Christiaan Barnard, 1960s heart transplant pioneer, with patient.*

The first transplants of human organs such as the kidney date back to the 1950s. In the 1960s, Dr. Christiaan Barnard broke new ground with heart transplant surgery in South Africa.

The idea seemed straightforward. If someone had a faulty kidney, heart, or other body organ, it could be replaced with a healthy one. In the early days, very little was known about how the body treats strange cells. Not until transplants were done did doctors discover that the defense cells of a healthy body treat a transplanted organ as an enemy and attack it fiercely.

▶ *This is not a picture of an alien invader, but a microscopic view of a macrophage cell, part of the body's clean-up system. Macrophages surround and digest foreign bodies, such as bacteria, as well as disposing of old cells.*

This 'immunodefense' reaction is exactly what your body does when you have a cold, for example. Your body's defenses rush to kill the cold germs. This type of reaction becomes a problem when a new heart or other organ gets attacked in the same way.

The pioneers of transplant technology developed drugs to reduce or stop these defenses. With the aid of such drugs, patients with transplanted organs have lived for many years. Genetic engineering could make organ transplanting even easier.

Old red blood cell about to be absorbed by macrophage

Macrophage is smaller than this dot

▶ Pigs, whose organs are used for human transplants, are known as 'transgenic' animals. The pigs are raised on laboratory farms where they are kept in totally virus-free conditions.

One idea is to use pigs as donors, because their internal organs are similar in size to human organs. By adding human genes to pig cells, scientists hope to create organs which human bodies will not reject. Researchers are concerned, however, that certain pig diseases could be passed on to humans.

Researchers fear that using animals as organ donors may pass animal diseases on to humans

Another transplant possibility may be tissue engineering. A small piece of tissue from a transplant patient or a relative, is used as a building block for growing cloned cells. Skin and cartilage have been grown this way, but growing more complex organs is still quite difficult. Some researchers have been trying to grow a liver. They hope to create tissue that is genetically engineered to be accepted by a body's defenses. The result may be 'cell banks,' in which replacement organs are grown to order.

▼ Body parts may one day be grown to order. In this futuristic view, the structure of a heart (seen on the video screens) has been made in plastic materials. This plastic heart is seeded with cloned muscle, blood vessels, nerves, and other cells. As the cells divide and the new heart grows, the plastic gradually dissolves, and its remains are carried away by pumps.

Where do organs come from?

Transplants are now very common. Figures for 1996, for example, show that 20,000 operations were carried out in the United States alone.

Spare organs are sometimes donated by living donors. A close relative may give a kidney. Most transplant organs, however, result from someone's misfortune, usually a fatal accident. A person who is dead, but with organs in good condition, makes a perfect organ donor. In some countries, people may carry a 'donor card' giving permission for their organs to be removed after death.

There is a trade in organs in India, where about 2000 people a year sell one of their two kidneys because they need the money.

Gene therapy

▲ *The first steps in public health care included building sewers. In 1870, a boat trip through the new sewer system of Paris was a big attraction!*

Experts believe gene therapy is a big leap forward in the treatment of disease. With this new medical technology, perfect genes can be inserted into human cells to correct diseases that might otherwise be incurable.

So far, there have been three big steps in treating disease. The first was public health works, such as providing clean water supplies and efficient disposal of toilet waste. The second was anesthetic surgery, which allowed a wide range of operations. The third was the vaccines and antibiotics that let doctors treat many diseases spread by microbes. Gene therapy is a fourth step.

Many illnesses are the result of one or more genes not working properly. The faulty genes cause cells to make the wrong amount or type of protein, leaving the body open to all sorts of illness. The idea behind gene therapy is to deliver a gene into a patient's cells to cure a disease.

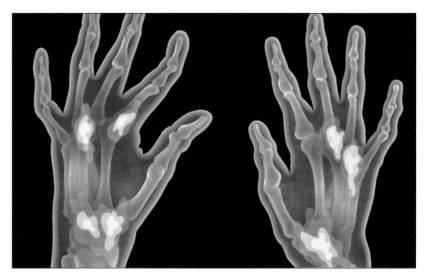

An early gene therapy patient was a young girl from the United States, Ashanti DeSilva. Ashanti inherited a defective gene from both parents, giving her a condition that left her body unable to fight infections. She was very ill and left home only to visit doctors.

▲ *The crippling condition of arthritis could be relieved by gene therapy.*

When Ashanti was four years old, gene therapy was tried out as a cure. On September 14, 1990, a medical team took out some of her white blood cells, inserted normal genes into them, and then returned the cells to her body.

◄ *The second big step in treating disease. A doctor uses anesthetic gas to make a patient unconscious before an operation in 1885. Without it, surgery had been a grim and painful experience.*

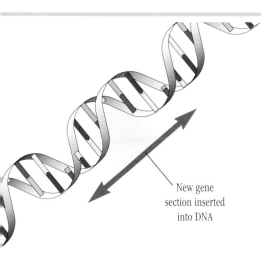

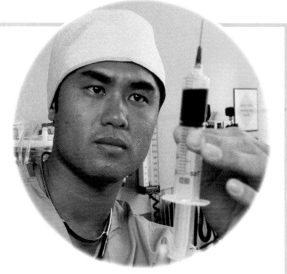

▶ *In the future, gene therapy may mean injections of genes directly into the bloodstream. The genes could be aimed at target cells (cancer cells, for example) while ignoring others. Once there, the new genetic material would order the patient's body to make a helpful protein to kill the dangerous cells.*

New gene
section inserted
into DNA

▲ *New genes are joined to DNA inside a cell. Cells carrying the repaired DNA are then ready to be returned to the body.*

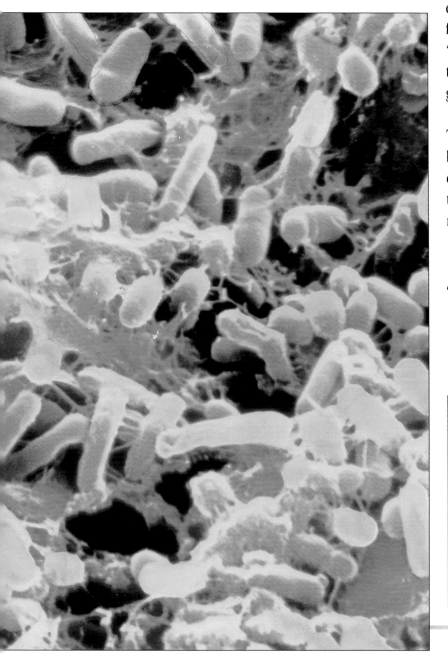

Over the next few months, Ashanti received more 'corrected' genes, and her health started to improve. The new genes had turned on her immune system, allowing her body's natural defenses to go to work and fight microbes from the outside world. Ashanti needs 'booster' treatments from time to time, but the gene therapy proved a great success.

Through the 1990s, other patients have been given gene therapy for other disorders. Many specialists are convinced that this treatment will become a normal medical practise.

◀ *Bacteria, such as these shown enlarged over 4000 times, are typical body attackers. The body's white blood cells, the 'antibodies,' are a defense force designed to destroy the invaders.*

Can genes cure diseases?

The potential is there to cure diseases and disorders. There are 5000 or more types of single gene disorders.

Cystic fibrosis is an inherited lung disease that kills most sufferers before they are 30 years old.

The gene that causes this disease was located in 1989. Four years later, a possible cure was tried out, with corrective genes breathed in through a nose spray. The tests were encouraging and work continues.

Genetic farming

▲ *Young 'Flavr Savr' tomato plants. This genetically modified food was first put on sale in 1994. The changes allowed fruit to ripen without softening.*

I n the 1960s, a 'green revolution' produced bumper crops by introducing new types of plants and herbicides to kill insect pests. Now genetic engineering is changing farming and food production around the world.

Today, genetic engineers are working on a new green revolution. Crops are being designed to have a better chance of survival against pests.

Some of these improvements will help farmers, but the big food companies may benefit most. They are moving fast to control the complete chain of food production, from seeds planted in the soil to the breakfast cereal in your bowl.

▶ *Genetically modified crops promise good yields, with fewer chemical sprays needed to eliminate pests, but some people still say traditional ways of growing are better.*

▲ *Genetic foods have become big business. For example, Europe buys up to 40 percent of the U.S. soya bean crop, of which nearly one-third is genetically modified.*

O ne genetically engineered product is the 'terminator' seed. This super-seed is disease-resistant and can produce bumper crops. However, farmers must buy a new supply every year, because the seed grows only once. Seeds cannot be harvested and saved for future use. For the seed company, 'terminator' seeds mean greater sales. For the farmer, it means spending more on seed.

Across the world, about $400 billion is spent on food production every year. In 1995, about $450 million was spent on genetically engineered seed, a sum that may grow 15 times or more by 2005. Not everyone agrees that genetically changed foods are without problems. Some people think super-seeds may end traditional farming methods.

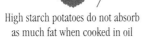

▶ Genetically modified fruit and vegetables are already on supermarket shelves. This group shows just a few planned changes to familiar foods.

Herbicide-resistant corn is already grown. Healthier cooking oil that uses low-fat corn is now being developed

Genetically modified cheese suitable for vegetarians is available now. It uses a special enzyme, rather than rennet, which comes from calves' stomachs

Genetically altered broccoli is a cancer fighter

Flavr Savr tomatoes have been in grocery stores since 1994. Further work could produce fruits that help fight cancer

High starch potatoes do not absorb as much fat when cooked in oil

An antifreeze protein from a cold-water fish may allow strawberries to be grown in cold climates

Bananas could in the future contain a vaccine against the liver disease hepatitis B. Slower ripening could improve taste

◀▶ A growing human population in the 21st century will make better food production important. Climate change may cause drought (left). Accidental fires may ruin crops (right).

Some experts believe there may be unknown dangers with genetically changed crops. Switzerland, Austria, and Luxembourg are among the countries that turn away products that include genetically modified organisms (GMO). "It's a risk that even the best scientist cannot predict," warned one scientist in 1998. The deadly disease BSE, or mad cow disease, which resulted partly from feeding ground-up meat remains to cattle, is a reminder that experts can make mistakes.

Despite these fears, genetic engineers may come up with some very tempting ideas. On the planning list are 'nutraceutical' products that are a cross between food and medicine. They include tomatoes that can protect against bowel problems, and vegetables with extra vitamins.

???
What is on the plate for genetic farming?

Food companies interested in GMO, or genetically modified products, spend a great deal of money persuading people that the new technology is safe.

People who object to the products do not have as much money to spend, so they compete by staging demonstrations and meetings, hoping to catch the attention of the world's news media.

Examples include protesters in Ireland uprooting GMO test crops, and Germans preventing the planting of some GMO sugar beets. In Britain, one action group visits supermarkets and marks packages of GMO food with a big 'X.'

Into the future

▲ *Genetically improved and cloned people might be living in the 21st century.*

Genetic engineering will be one of the most important areas of scientific progress in the future. What does the future hold for genetic engineering?

Cloning technology has already moved ahead by leaps and bounds. It took only two years after Dolly the sheep was created for researchers to clone other mammals. Research in human cloning is progressing, too. Soon, this type of genetic engineering could be an option for people who cannot otherwise have children. However, many people are worried about the problems this new technology will bring.

▶ *In the future, genetic weapons may be more dangerous than nuclear bombs. Scientists could create diseases that are more deadly than the Black Death of the Middle Ages. Just a teaspoon of the worst plague germs could wipe out most of the people in a major city.*

For other fields of genetic engineering, the future is a whole new frontier. Gene therapy has already helped many people fight disease. Researchers are also investigating the possibility of using some animals as organ donors for humans.

By genetically engineering plants, seed companies have already created 'super-seeds' that grow plentiful crops but also change traditional ways of life. Genetic engineering could create flowers that have strange new color patterns and plants that are altered to produce oil for vehicle fuels.

◀ *By 2020, a flower-show winner may be the GMO 'super-stripe' rose, a possible outcome of early-1990s Dutch experiments, when petunias were grown with petals covered with rings and splashes of color.*

In 1998, a gene was found that may unlock the secrets of aging. Lifespans vary widely in nature – bristlecone pines live 5000 years or more, but an adult mayfly may last just one day. Humans vary in lifespan, too. The oldest recorded person (Jeanne Calmet, right) lived for 122 years. Some researchers believe that one day people may lead an active life to this sort of age, instead of today's more usual 70-80 years.

Huge tusks and shaggy coats mark out mammoths from their elephant relatives

Mammoths became extinct over 10,000 years ago, perhaps because of hunting by humans

Woolly mammoths may be brought back to life using cloning technology. Pandas, tigers, and other endangered species may also be rescued from extinction this way.

▲ *The future? A young 'mammophant' (left) with its elephant mother.*

I t may be possible to bring some prehistoric animals back to life. Researchers plan to find a frozen woolly mammoth in icy-cold Siberia. They will use DNA from a mammoth sperm cell to fertilize the egg of a distantly related modern elephant. By painstakingly adjusting the genes through several generations, it is hoped eventually to have an almost 'pure bred' mammoth.

While this is not quite so dramatic as the dinosaurs of the Jurassic Park movies, wildlife parks of the future may have some interesting 'new' animals.

Can cloning save animals?

Maybe, says Professor Chen Dayuan. He is a Chinese scientist eager to save the rare giant panda, of which there are fewer than 1000 left in the wild.

Professor Dayuan plans to insert cells from an adult panda into another animal's egg from which the DNA has been removed. That animal (probably a dog) will go on to give birth to a baby panda.

In New Zealand, the disappearing Auckland Island cattle breed was saved from extinction in 1998. By similar methods as were used to clone Dolly the sheep, a cloned calf was born.

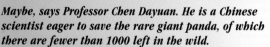

Time track

A list of some important dates in genetic research, from the work of pioneer botanists to the first transplant of a human organ.

▲ *By the 1990s, plants were genetically modified for all sorts of reasons.*

▲ *Alfred Wallace was an English naturalist who came up with ideas similar to Charles Darwin's. The two lectured together in 1858.*

1608 Zacharias Jansen from Holland invents the microscope, an instrument that reveals the universe in miniature. For the first time, people can see the details of tiny living things, such as insects and plants.

1665 English scientist Robert Hooke publishes Micrographia, the first book based on observations made using a microscope. In the book, Hooke tells how he looked at a slice of cork and saw that it was made of "many little boxes." He calls them cells, and scientists will show later that all living things are made up of cells.

1735 Botanist Carl Linnaeus from Sweden publishes System of Nature. The book sorts living things into plant and animal kingdoms. Linnaeus also starts the two-part Latin naming system still used today. An example is Homo sapiens. 'Homo' is the family of man, while 'sapiens' is our particular type and means 'thinking.'

1822 Gregor Mendel born. The modern science of genetics dates from his work in the gardens of the monastery at Brno, in what is now the Czech Republic. After experimenting for many years, he forms his laws of inheritance. These enable researchers to predict what characteristics – height, color, and so on – can be expected in new generations of living things.

1831 Charles Darwin from England sets out as ship's naturalist on HMS Beagle, on a mission to survey the coast of South America. During mainland visits on the five-year voyage, Darwin finds many fossils, showing that some animal species die out while others continue to breed and flourish. On the isolated Galapagos Islands, far out in the Pacific Ocean, Darwin discovers groups of finches with different-shaped beaks, a puzzle he is determined to solve.

1831 Scottish botanist Robert Brown investigates cells with a microscope and sees that they all have a tiny speck inside. He labels this object the 'nucleus,' a Latin word meaning 'little nut.'

1838 German botanist Matthias Schlieden studies many plants and sees that they are all made from cells.

1838 Karl von Nageli, a Swiss botanist, sees how a cell divides into tiny strands, later called 'chromosomes.'

1859 Charles Darwin's On the Origin of Species is published. He claims that living things may change naturally, according to changes in their environment. Darwin also suggests the idea of evolution from simpler forms of life millions of years in the past. Many people are upset by this and by Darwin's suggestion of apes as human ancestors. Religious teachings have said that life on Earth was created only a few thousand years ago, with humanity being the highest form of life.

1865 Gregor Mendel's studies are published in the journal of the Brno Natural Scientific Society. It is largely ignored until it is rediscovered in 1900 by Hugo de Vries, from Holland. De Vries also puts forward the idea of evolution moving in sudden jumps, by 'mutation.'

1907 Experimental work is begun by American Thomas Hunt Morgan. He produces the first 'chromosome map,' showing the location of genes. His tests use fruit flies because of their simple genetic structure and rapid breeding.

1932 First electron microscope made by two German engineers Ernst Ruska and Max Knoll. It uses beams of electron particles instead of light rays.

1953 American James Watson and Francis Crick from England determine the shape and structure of the DNA molecule, shown as a 'double helix,' or double spiral. DNA is the carrier of the genetic code common to all forms of life on Earth.

◀▶ *In 1838, Matthias Schlieden found that all plants are made of cells. At left a cactus, at right a convolvulus.*

1960s   Organ transplants started by Dr. Christiaan Barnard in South Africa. His work reveals problems created by the body's natural defenses, notably the rejection of foreign tissues.

1960s   The first 'green revolution.' Crops are bred for better growth. New chemicals designed to kill crop-wrecking insects are mostly successful, but many insects develop resistance to chemicals.

1973   Two U.S. researchers, Herbert Boyer and Stanley Cohen, experiment with 'recombinant DNA.' They slide out sections of DNA from different bacteria, rejoining them to form a new strand of DNA.

1980   First patent granted on a living thing – a microorganism designed to digest waste created by spills from tankers at sea or from offshore oil rigs.

1988   Special type of mouse patented for use in research projects.

1990   Gene therapy used to treat a patient with a poor immune defense system. Injections with undamaged DNA boost the body's ability to resist disease and let the patient lead a normal life.

1990   Human Genome Organization (HUGO) involves thousands of scientists across the world. Its aim is to map out all the genes in human DNA by 2005. It is estimated there are 80-100,000 of them.

1994   First genetically modified food, the 'Flavr Savr' tomato, goes into supermarkets. Modifications allow the tomato to ripen on the vine without softening. The modified fruit are also less likely to be damaged when being transported.

1994   Second green revolution begins, with genetically modified organism (GMO) crops being planted.

1994   First 'genetic crime.' Two men are caught by police after stealing cells from a U.S. laboratory and trying to sell them for $300,000. The cells contain a gene that could be useful in helping combat failing human kidneys.

1996   Dolly the sheep cloned by a team based in Edinburgh, Scotland. They strip a cell of its genetic material and put fresh DNA into it, resulting in a clone. Dolly is the first mammal to be cloned.

1997   Researchers at the University of Bath in England, create headless tadpoles. Possible future uses for the technology include tissue banks, where spare organs can be grown as replacements.

1998   Scientists at the University of Hawaii create 22 mouse clones, using similar methods as those used for Dolly the sheep. The researchers also create clones of the clones, and say they could produce up to 200 mouse clones a day.

1998   Experiments with cell-repair genes show that it may be possible to extend the human lifespan by 40 percent. Researchers say that people could still be active and largely free of the diseases of old age.

1998   A disappearing breed of New Zealand cattle is cloned by 'nuclear transfer,' the same method as used for Dolly the sheep in 1996. This marks the dawn of cloning to save endangered species. Other ideas include bringing back to life extinct animals, such as the woolly mammoth.

Beyond 2000
The Human Genome Organization completes the map of human chromosome.

Pigs raised in laboratory conditions used as organ donors. This follows the earlier use of pigs to supply heart valves.

First human clones.

Tissue banks become common, with organs grown to order in the laboratory.

Genetic screening for defects becomes a standard check for pregnant mothers.

Active human lifespan of 120-150 years becomes possible as researchers find out the secrets of cell repair and many diseases of old age.

'Alpha humans' are created, with reduced number of genetic defects, superior intelligence, and resistance to disease.

Human genetic modifications and cloning become common.

▲ In 1980, a microorganism was created to help clean up oil spills.

▲ The microscope was invented in the early 1600s. This model dates from the 1870s.

Glossary

An explanation of technical terms and concepts.

▲ *Fossil remains of an ammonite, an ancient sea creature.*

Amino acids
Units that make up all the proteins in living organisms. Green plants can make all of these organic acids they need. Animals must eat nutrient-rich food to provide all the amino acids necessary for building tissues.

Arthritis
Painful inflammation of the joints. It is usually a condition that comes with age.

Bacteria
Single-cell organisms that reproduce by dividing. Many types cause diseases, but other bacteria, such as the those that change milk to yogurt, are very useful.

Cell
Smallest living unit. Some simple organisms are single cells. Most plants and animals are made of many cells of different shapes and sizes. Typically, a cell consists of a watery, jelly-like substance called 'cytoplasm,' surrounded by a membrane that gives the cell its shape. Various things enter through this cell wall, including oxygen and food. Waste products pass the other way. Tiny chemical factories in the cell, called 'organelles,' produce enzymes and other substances useful to the body (see Enzyme).

Cell division
In simple organisms, a cell, including the nucleus, divides by splitting in half. In complex organisms, a process called 'mitosis' ensures the genes are shared. 'Meiosis' is the way male and female sex cells – sperm and eggs – are formed.

Chromosome
Microscopic threads inside the nucleus of a cell that carry DNA and genes. Humans have 22 pairs of chromosomes plus a pair that determine sex. We all have the same number of chromosomes, but our slightly different genes make us individuals.

Clone
Living creature made from a single cell without sexual reproduction. The new organism is genetically identical to the parent. In humans, a 'natural' clone is an identical twin, where the egg has split after fertilization, separating into two embryos that have the same genes.

DNA
Abbreviation for deoxyribonucleic acid, the molecule that makes up chromosomes and genes. It is shaped as two long spiral threads, coiled around each other.

Egg
Sex cell made by a female animal. After fertilization, the egg (or ovum) divides into more cells to become an embryo. In birds, developing chicks feed on the yolk until they are big enough to hatch. A female mammal's egg is not laid like a bird's. A developing embryo gets its food from the mother's body until birth.

Electron microscope
Type of microscope with strong magnifying power. A beam of electrons is fired on a subject, then focused by a powerful magnetic system. The result is shown on a video screen, and photographed.

Embryo
Name for the early stages of a fertilized egg, as it divides and grows. At eight weeks, a human embryo is barely an inch (25.4 mm) long, though it has the beginnings of arms, legs, and eyes. In later development, an embryo is usually called a 'fetus.'

Enzyme
A substance, made of protein and produced by a cell, that speeds up various processes. A typical cell may have up to 100,000 different enzymes, needed for various jobs. Examples of these include enzymes that convert food to simple

➡ **KINGDOM**	***Animalia***	Animals
➡ **PHYLUM**	***Chordata***	Animals with backbones
➡ **CLASS**	***Mammalia***	Mammals
➡ **ORDER**	***Carnivora***	Meat eaters
➡ **FAMILY**	***Felidae***	Cats
➡ **GENUS**	***Panthera***	Panthers, group of similar species
➡ **SPECIES**	***Tigris***	Tiger

◀ *How to classify a species, using the system first developed by Carl Linnaeus (1707-1778). Organisms are placed into smaller and smaller groupings, down to species. A species is a group of animals that can breed with each other over several generations. Species may evolve or change over time, if their genes adapt to a changing environment. Mutations may also create changes.*

◀ *Panthera tigris.*

substances for digestion. Other enzymes link simple substances together to form more complex ones.

Evolution
The theory that existing species developed from earlier forms of life. 'Natural selection' is a part of evolution theory. It means that creatures change in ways that best suit survival in particular environments. Creatures not suited to the environment will die. Evolution can also happen through mutation (see Mutation).

Extraterrestrial
Literally, 'out of the Earth.' Normally used to describe life (even simple organisms) on other planets.

Fertilization
Meeting of sex cells, such as male sperm and female egg during reproduction. When sex cells join together, DNA from each is mixed, and egg cells divide and grow to form an embryo.

Fossil
Hardened, or 'petrified,' stone-like remains of a living thing that died millions of years ago. Fossils of many prehistoric plants and animals have been found, from sea creatures (see picture top left, opposite) to giant dinosaurs.

Gene
Coded message stored along the DNA of a chromosome. Gene sequences provide the pattern for life – from the size of your foot, to the color of your hair.

Gene therapy
Medical treatment that injects perfect genes into the cells of a patient to 'switch on' the patient's own defective genes.

Genetic engineering
Changing the genes of a living thing in the laboratory. Genes are taken from one set of genes to another using enzymes that act as 'scissors' to cut up a DNA molecule.

Genome
All the genes in a cell. Each type of living thing has its own genome, ranging from simple ones in flies to the complex ones in humans and other mammals.

GMO
Short for genetically modified organism. A GMO might be anything from a strain of disease-resistant wheat to a mouse that has been genetically engineered for laboratory tests.

Hydra
Small freshwater creature with a tube-shaped body and mouth surrounded by tentacles. Hydras reproduce 'asexually' – by budding. The young are clones of the parent hydra.

Immune system
Body defense against infections. 'Antibodies,' produced by white blood cells, attack invading bacteria and viruses.

Mammal
Animal that is warm-blooded, gives birth to live young, and feeds its babies with mother's milk. Examples include sheep, cows, cats, dogs, and humans.

Molecule
Group of atoms arranged in various ways. A molecule of water is made of two hydrogen atoms and one of oxygen. DNA molecules are very complex, ranging from 100,000 to 10 million atoms, depending on the organism.

Mutation
Sudden change in a gene. Most mutations are harmful in some way and result in early death, but some may be useful and get passed on to new generations.

Nucleus
The life center of a cell, containing DNA. Genetic instructions carried by the DNA control the way the body works.

Protein
Organic compound found in living things, made from chains of amino acids. There are thousands of proteins, each with a different job. Body parts such as muscles are made almost entirely of protein.

Rejection
Non-acceptance by the body of organs transplanted from another person or an animal. The body's immune system treats the new tissue as an invader.

Species
A group of living things that can breed among themselves (see table on opposite page) and have young that can do the same. Some species are close enough to each other to breed, but the young cannot continue to reproduce. A mule is an example of this. It is an animal that results from fertilization between a donkey and a horse but cannot have young itself.

Transplant
The transfer during special surgery of a healthy organ, such as a heart or kidney, from one body to another.

Virus
Tiny organism that usually causes disease in animals and plants. A virus invades a cell, turning it into a virus production center. Then the cell bursts and dies, releasing the new viruses to spread to other cells. Viruses are parasites that need a host cell in which to live.

Womb
Another word for the female uterus, the part of the body in which an embryo develops.

▲ There is a great variety of life on earth. Yet, all species are thought to have a common ancestor that thrived nearly four billion years ago, when the first lifeforms developed.

Index

Acknowledgements
We wish to thank all those individuals and organizations that have helped us create this publication:

Photographs supplied by:
Alpha Archive
A. Barrington Brown
Bruce Coleman Collection
Cellmark Diagnostics
Celltech Ltd.
Chris Bjornberg
C.C. Lockwood
Columbia TriStar Films (UK)
Corbis UK Ltd
D. Phillips
Dr. Gopal Murti
Dr. Linda Stannard, UCT
Dr. Yorgos Nikas
Eurelios
Institut Pasteur/CNRI
James Holmes
J.C. Revy
Mary Evans Picture Library
Mary Plage
Maximilian Stock Ltd.
New Scientist
Peter Menzel
Professor K. Seddon and Dr. T. Evans, Queen's University, Belfast
Catherine Pouedras
Hans Reinhard
Science Photo Library
Kim Taylor
Telegraph Colour Library
The Kobal Collection
Topham Picturepoint
L. Willatt, East Anglian Regional Genetics Service

Digital art created by:
David Jefferis
Gavin Page/Design Shop

Further assistance from:
Michael Gerr and his pigs